# Life in lo

## Musings from a Kentish Hamlet in lockdown

by John F Bennett
Illustrations by Jessica Hayes

Preface

When the first news of Covid 19 broke in China, it was clear this terrible virus would eventually affect the whole world. With global mobility through air travel, it would only be days before the first cases arrived in the UK.

Sadly, my prediction came true and based on the information coming out of the Far East, it was obvious that those with pre-existing illnesses would be vulnerable. My wife Sue, is susceptible to asthma and the thought of this compounding the virus gave us cause for some concern.

We decided to self-isolate in early March, well before the Government guidelines were issued, we had full freezers etc left over from Christmas, when we were too poorly to eat!

We made the necessary arrangements and settled in for the long haul. I know many ex-service individuals who wouldn't cope with isolation very well and decided to create a focus. As a veteran myself, I work with the local regimental association as the Mental Health Champion, giving support to those who have seen and done things that civilians just can't understand or comprehend.

I decided to write a daily blog for social media which these individuals follow quite avidly. It needed to be truthful with an element of embroidery, but encompassing terms they would understand and relate to.

After it started it was clear that my civilian friends waited expectantly for the daily ramblings, so again, I changed the approach slightly. Writing the blog was for me, quite therapeutic and the thought of supporting others drove me to continue. Unfortunately, I encountered technical problems, and together with a detached retina, there are gaps I hopefully managed to make up and engage my readers.

On the 8th of May, the 75th anniversary of VE day, I posted an excerpt of one of my books. My uncle was killed in the invasion of Crete and I felt it was a poignant reminder of those dark times in our proud but chequered history.

There is a glossary of terms at the end of the book to explain some of the jargon I used, in the hope it makes sense!

When the 'stay at home' instruction was lifted and the 'stay alert' message was given I decided to conclude the blog. We visited the farm shops and the various outlets for supplies at the most obscure times, to avoid other people and so far, this has worked.

At the time of writing, we seem to be coming out of this but we should exercise caution. All the great pandemics in history have come back for a second wave.

Please enjoy this book, the contents are very loosely based on characters and events unfolding during periods of extreme boredom.

John F Bennett,  March 2021

Dedicated to;

All those in the front line and our elected representatives who have had to make some difficult and unprecedented decisions.

Our friends and family who we haven't seen for months!

All the individuals mentioned hoping they will speak to me again!

Day 1.

*The stores are ready, fresh water in, no external visits planned, let's see how it goes!*

Day 2.

*It's been a long night, I have been down to the local army training area with a head torch, metal detector and a shovel. Back in 1979, the army boss man bought everyone fish and chips for supper so we didn't need the tins of steak, cheese possessed, nor the tins of fruit pudding.*

*We couldn't take them back to barracks or the quartermaster would get very cross! We buried them...*

*Fast forward forty two years, I couldn't find them anywhere! I found a mortar bomb from 1942, boxes of blank ammunition and a complete Mark 1(Mk1) land rover. Not sure what we will eat today!*

*Day 3.*

*I thought this isolation thing was going to be problematical but having pulled out the tent, camping cookers and of course camp beds (age thing you know!) we realised that we still have gas, electricity and our log burner so we don't feel the need to camp in the garden just yet.*

*This is getting serious, local pub has had most of its bookings cancelled for Mother's Day and beyond.*

*I need to negotiate beer take away's asap. Hens are laying so this will negate the need for toilet roll so watch out on eBay in a few days, fifty quid a roll is the going rate.*

*Holiday plans in full flow, this year we are going to holiday local. I think a week in the conservatory will be a welcome change, Alexa will come too so we have music!*

*Day 4.*

*Bit of a quiet day, found the Monopoly box I bought in 1983, the film wrapper was stuck on but after a bit of struggling opened the box and set it up.*

*Clearly it was out of date, the house prices were set in the 1960s. We spend the rest of the day with a felt tip pen to add realistic inflation.*

*When we finally started playing the dog decided to jump on it and everything went up in the air!*

*Back in the day long life milk did what it said, you could buy it with a two year sell by date, now it's two months! The roads are quiet, it's a bit like Christmas day without rellies clutching presents!*

*Not as many delivery vehicles around as I would have expected, but we haven't actually ordered anything yet! Today going to deep clean cupboards and drawers to see what is out of date, I do know there is a huge jar of sauerkraut in the top cupboard I bought in 1994, tentatively going to check if edible as I have a ten-year-old tin of bratwurst to go with it.*

*Forgive me for this but it's time for a Bennett rant, I have witnessed first-hand the greed, stupidity and utter selfishness of a certain age of shoppers in the supermarkets over the last few days.*

*The problem is simple in my view. We don't have enough wars to focus us to look after the elderly, infirm and families. In the early 1900s, the Boer war was fought* and the repercussions went far and wide. The country stuck together and worked it out.

The children of the Boer war veterans remembered these hard times, and brought up their children to remember and adapt accordingly.

In 1914 it started again, the process was repeated and children heard constantly first-hand what it was like to see hardship. Skip forward to 1940 and the children of the previous generation went to fight.

You can see where this is going can't you? In 1945 they all came home and their children were reminded often of the hardship and how they overcome crisis. (I was one of these children!)

Same again in Korea, but after that wars were not so big and didn't affect as many people. We brought our children up correctly but having no first-hand experience of the tough times, they have become selfish and greedy in an age where so much is available, and information is too readily on tap.

We should have had another full-scale war in 1960 and things would be a damn sight different. I am feeling ashamed to be British at the moment and fear for the next generation. The sight of elderly shoppers trying to buy essentials brings a tear to my eye, there is enough for everyone, it's incredibly selfish and in poor taste.

If it was one of their grandparents would they shove them out of the way for a tin of beans? Sadly, yes, I think they would.

Day 5.

Interesting day yesterday, watched the chaos on TV with mindless inconsiderate morons shopping. My parents would have been disgusted in the behaviour displayed. On a lighter note, I have cut up some sticks to help start the log burner and this gave me an idea.

We have bandit's about at night locally, some people still have to nick other people's things, so it gave me a thought. Why not whittle down the sticks and create a punji stick barrier at the end of the garden?

Wipe liberally with some chicken poo and hey presto, instant defences! It's got legs will think harder on this, on a different subject, we blew out the monopoly thingy, I don't have a particularly good financial acumen, my track record of buying and selling houses is not that great.

I ended up with all the slum roads and kept going to jail, if only I had bought the utilities and made a killing on their share prices when this all blows over!

TV flicking and getting concerned this morning, BBC2 has songs of praise in full flow, you can't beat a few hymns to blow out the cobwebs but at 06:35 the neighbour has just started beating on the wall in perfect timing. This could catch on!

Right, time for breakfast and back to the sticks, the shavings will be useful for the smoker, there is nothing better than smoked bacon grill with a lightly fried egg!

Day 6.

Interesting day today, been in contact with many of my 'old military compatriots' today checking if they are ok and sorted for supplies, I have many, so it took most of the day. However, the routine here carries on.

The Monopoly is in the recycling bin and we have now set up a small table in the lounge. We have the chess set out and will play a game or two later. I am a little nervous over this as although I was team captain of the chess club in 1972, I haven't played since.

My wife Sue, is an expert so I must resist playing for money or removal of clothing, now there is a thought?

I have now a domain name and a website thingy, I am a real numpty in these matters so I expect I will end up advertising Sellotape and not my new book!

My biggest challenge will be to arrange beer, now the pub has shut I will have to use a bit of ingenuity, I have arranged that if we connect up the hosepipe to the doombar pump, and I have the other end in a bucket in the kitchen, with clever use of a two way radio I can get beer delivered via the pipe. I can run a tab and settle up later.

All ready to go but one minor problem as the beer started to flow it pumped through all the water in the pipe complete with earwigs, slugs and a disgruntled spider.

Oh well plan B bottled water then! This isolation thingy is certainly interesting I have in plan to clean the mud from the hen's feet tomorrow!


Day 7.

Busy day, it's lucky we have some good weather. The task of the day was completed without some degree of drama. The hens saw me coming armed with all the gear! I caught the big one first who shouted and flapped nonstop until I upended her!

Washing mud off their feet is quite therapeutic and subconsciously I began to hum Hotel California to myself, out of the corner of my eye I noticed the other hens were *bobbing their heads along with the time. You couldn't write about it!*

*The cleaning went well but she didn't like the claw cream after the task was complete, walked off muttering about nail polish.*

*The process was repeated with the others, and after getting through Life in the Fast lane, Two Bridges Road and finally Desperado, they all sat there gently rocking and tapping their nicely clean claws on the decking! Who would have believed they were so conversant with the songs of The Eagles!*

*Grateful as always, they only laid two eggs instead of the normal six!*

*I am guilty as charged, yes, I hoarded. I really like Taylors Christmas blend coffee. Some years it's everywhere but in 2018 there wasn't any in the local supermarkets. In 2019 it was in the shops from October so I gradually stocked up and was very proud of my thirty-nine packets.*

*Yesterday, I opened the last one! From now on I will be twitching with withdrawal symptoms and be very, very grumpy! Social distancing is working well in our house, Sue is on one sofa, the dog is on the other and I am on the floor! I think we have this sorted! Bacon sandwich time!*

Day 8.

*Interesting day today, my neighbour who plays golf six or seven days a week unless he is on death's door, is clearly under curfew and had his pass revoked.*

*He has polished his bicycle which he hasn't rode for seventeen years, pressure washing the pavement outside the house which is covered in green mould, (from our oak tree I might add) our joint brick path is now spotless especially between the gaps. Sterling job sir but I fear that is it, boredom has truly set in.*

*A DPD (knock on your door and run-away man) van just delivered a square box which looks like one of those indoor golf putting things, which bounces your ball back after it hit the target. No movement outside in two hours, the kit and pressure washer are abandoned on the pavement... While he has been titting about I have read an email from the council stating the green waste bins are not being emptied for the foreseeable future. He has just loaded his green bin with three quarters of its size with my wet moss!!!*

*Having some inspiration from the gardener next door, we have counted all the plant pots over wintering in the shed, and have discovered we have three times more than actually have something alive in them, (not counting the tiger slugs and spiders) a job for later in the week will be to wash and size them in colour order!*

*I thought this isolation thing would be boring, but far from it, always something mad going on around here.*

*We are pushing the boat out for supper tonight, from the back of the cupboard one our favourite meals when camping I might add, is tinned stewed steak, instant mash and tinned peas! The recent supplies stock check revealed we had several in hand. The one for tonight has a best before 1987 date so well matured!*

*We have managed to project the laptop to the television screen, there is a live web cam on the beach at the British Virgin Islands. Gentle breeze blowing the palm trees with the occasional catamaran drifting by.*

*Very relaxing but in three days we have not seen one virgin! Oh well time to fire up the cooker and mess tins!*

Day 9.

*We decided to give ourselves a day off today. Up at daybreak and stocked the logs for the log burner, the news of the lockdown was not unexpected but joe public's take on this is beyond belief.*

*I have just witnessed someone I know going for a run, not unusual in itself but he hasn't been for a run in thirty years!*

*'Exercise once a day run or walk' Bloody sheep! Baa Baa Baa! If it was raining, we wouldn't see anyone out.*

*In the mindset of being on two weeks holiday, very hot in conservatory so time to break out the St Lucia suitcase, shorts and Caribbean shirt, good old Alexa is playing 'Kingston town' to get us in the spirit of things. Fortunately, we have many bottles of rum so it's rum punch over ice when the sun hit's the yardarm later! The book 'Hell in by Head' is confirmed for release on 30 July by the Conrad press, very exciting, just working with a designer to get the front cover as good as it could be!*

*Watching the news this morning it's clear the gene pool needs a bit of thinning oh dear! What are people like.*

*I also think that this not so good for a certain occupation, burglars will be out of work as everyone will be sitting in their castles!*

Day 10.

*It seems so quiet around here at the moment, everyone in the close are at home and no car movement out on the road.*

*Maybe this will be the answer so we can return to normal as soon as possible. One thing does worry me is the sheer stupidity of some people.*

*First food queuing after there was a piece on breakfast TV about behaving normally and people shouldn't panic buy or stockpile. What happens? three hours later the supermarkets are rammed, but instead of food, people have bought forty million toilet rolls! When you run out of food you won't need toilet rolls!*

*We are going to shut the pubs! two hours later the supermarket shelves are cleared of all the beer wine and spirits, some of which are so obscure I would never have heard of them! How weird?*

*The strangest thing is the closure of hairdressers, there was a run on the supermarkets again, this time for hair colour, ladies were so concerned they would have roots visible they bought whatever it was. I visualise ladies at home with purple hair, old codgers like me normally with a gentle shade of grey, walking around extremely ginger, it doesn't bear thinking about! Grey bearded, ginger hair and very grumpy! Can't get the picture out of my head!*

*Looking forward to supper, it's a baby's head mash and cabbage, may even bring it forward to lunchtime! For those balking at this statement, a baby's head isn't what it seems, its army speak for a tinned steak and kidney pudding in a tin.*

*The pastry is white due to the canning process. When it's upside down on a tray looks like it's nickname.*

*For those who read my memoirs, I should be sick to death of them but I absolutely love them! On the trips to Germany back in the early 1980s we used to stop at field rest areas for food and fuel frequently, but the only thing you could keep hot for long periods of time was the baby's head, tinned peas and powdered mash! I commend it to everyone even just the once!*

*Hen house deep clean today, they want their work surfaces deep cleaned and their garden furniture washed! Bloody hens, they think they own the joint!*

Day 11.

*Those pesky hens had me over yesterday, I was trying to clean them out and when I wasn't looking, they used me as a stepladder. One hop and they were in the garden and running around like birds possessed. It took over an hour to catch them. They rewarded me with zero eggs! I wonder what farmyard hens taste like?*

*I thought the list of tasks around the house would peter out but I think there is at least two weeks more to do. The garage needs sorting out, I found a mower yesterday I thought I had thrown in the skip five years ago, together with two bottles of the special edition Queen's regiment ale from about 2013.*

*The quest for my old army sleeping bag was finally ended today when it was discovered in a cardboard box.*

It also had a family of mice having a party throwing the sleeping bag lining at me with some abuse... They must have found the other bottle of beer!

The silence during the day is amazing, reminds me of childhood in the country when cars and machinery were few and far between. We are living in some odd and unprecedented times. Stay in and stay safe!

Day 13.

The end of the world has come, fact! I read today the ordering line and website for Laithwaites wine delivery has closed for the foreseeable future. This is getting bloody serious; we need wine and pretty quick!

The grapevines in the tubs are doing well, plenty of buds again this year, which going on previous years should produce thirty plus bunches like last year. Oh, how I wish we had made wine and not bloody grape jelly!

We have been in self-isolation for thirteen days now, there has to be a limit on how far we can eke out the alcohol. I am very lucky that my memory is a bit thin, I hid a bottle of doombar last week for emergencies and can't remember where!

I have found on the internet how to make rice wine but I am sceptical of its potency. We have four kilos of rice in stock so best foot forward!

We have been to the Caribbean quite a bit over the years and always come back with at least three litres of rum each time, two legal and one in the suitcase just for luck!

Oh, you lawbreaker I hear everyone yelling, toughtitty I say. This rum is not for drinking, we can't stand the stuff, tastes like cat wee, and believe me I know

16

*what that tastes like! No, it's for the fruit of the Christmas cakes, makes those little chaps go plump and squidgy and changes the flavour.*

*In my boredom yesterday I had a count up, we have one bottle with half used and forty-one bottles ready for action. For those mathematically adept we can make Christmas cakes for the next 212 years!*

*If by some chance I go quiet you will know I am sitting here watching war movies, stinking of cat wee and gently rocking!*

Day 14.

*Two weeks of being stuck in doors is taking its toll, I can't find the doombar beer anywhere and was getting desperate at 9pm. I have a memento of St Lucia, a single bottle of Piton beer.*

*For those who saw my Caribbean beer blog a few years ago, will realise that this is my number two favourite beer behind the ubiquitous Banks, with the others trailing behind in poor order. I popped said Piton in the freezer for a quick chill and prepared the glass (no bottle slugging for me now I am 63!)*

*We watched MasterChef and followed up with a couple of Hairy Bikers. and then after a hard day tending crops in the fields went to bed!*

*As usual the good old bladder bellowed at 3am and I remembered the beer! I rushed down and opened the freezer, but at the point of freezing the pressure had popped the lid off, and there was beer slush all over the contents of the freezer. I slunk off back upstairs for a fitful sleep knowing how much doodoo I would be in and of course, I was not disappointed!*

*This morning I have had to clean out the contents of the freezer under strict supervision! Oh and of course no bloody beer!*

*Thinking about the rum from yesterday, one of my friends read yesterday's missive and asked if he could blag a bottle from me? Are some people real? How am I going to get a bottle of rum to Peterborough? Is it me?*

*I have effectively been confined to barracks with an element of being in Coventry, my tinnitus is playing up today and the silence is somewhat deafening. Even Alexa won't talk to me this morning.*

*I need points and quick! I think I will be chopping logs in the garage for some time!*

Day 15.

*At my age you would have thought I would know where the safety catch was on my mouth. Bearing in mind I have already tainted the frozen fruit and pork chops, with one of the finest beers known to man.*

*I can't lift or shove much these days as the old back injury plays up and I have to be a bit careful, so when I hear 'the sofa is heavy', my first thought was if you put the Dyson down and use two hands it will slide, but no, it just came out. I just couldn't help it. 'put your back into it', Well that was it, Sue will do in the Olympic games next year with the long-distance Dyson throwing competition.*

*I swear it cleared my head by two feet, but on a positive note the adrenalin surge made the sofa slide out with ease!*

*Having thought I had got away with that I forgot that the flex has a three-pin-plug, as the machine crumpled into the conservatory, I caught the plug firmly* on the back of my head. Ouch! Anyway, everything has calmed down and I am back in the garage cutting more wood with three small plasters on my head...

That cool dude Levi Roots has a recipe for a Caribbean apple crumble which looks amazing. The normal crumble mixture contains twice the butter vs flour seriously rich. It's full of cinnamon, ground ginger and allspice, a marriage made in my cooker! Slight problem with this, anyone fancy doing a swop for some cooking apples for a litre of rum? Ps diet still going well!

Day 16.

Getting a bit stir crazy today the snow curtailed my wander around the garden, and certainly no garage duties. The Caribbean crumble worked with pineapple, but it would be better with clotted cream but custard isn't too bad. The recipe is on the internet, look for Levi Roots recipes. I can't recommend it enough!

I have eighty and a half bricks on the fireplace confirmed by counting five times. Crap on TV so reading a book by Fergal Keane about the siege of Kohima, that will keep me off the streets (metaphorically of course!)

Spent all day trying to speak to car insurance co who didn't auto renew my policy... three day wait with no insurance... GRRRRR

Day 16 - part two

*I thought I would for the record mention that I am having hen trouble again. They have decided to social distance themselves. I went in to get the eggs and there wasn't any at all.*

*After threats of roast lunch and feather duvets, they pointed out they had in fact done better than usual. There was one in each corner of the hen house and one in the dirt outside! They think they are funny! They are cackling and chuntering, laughing behind their wings and generally taking the micky!*

*They haven't realised that I have to top up their food tower today! They will laugh on the other side of their beaks when I delay it a day! Top tip, don't get hens, they will always have you over when you least expect it!*

Day 17.

*Well, the car insurance saga played out during the day. I had a call back from the call centre, it couldn't have been a more inconvenient time for them for this to happen.*

*All the staff are mostly working from home but there is a shortage of laptops, and those they have in the system did not get tested properly. All credit to their staff!*

*The chap on the end of the phone was extremely helpful, perhaps on my initial contact email mentioning that I was a shareholder helped a tad!!! So, it appears dumdum here pressed the wrong button when we changed the car last year. I accidentally pressed the button to cancel the auto renewal.*

*They had to set up a new policy which they did pretty quickly, whilst transferring the staff discounts and NCD. So, seven hours later I am now insured to drive my car which hasn't moved an inch for seventeen days! I do feel a bit bad now though, I have only thirteen shares in a top five Insurance company which I didn't buy, the share save scheme wasn't so good so I left it some years back.*

*When I retired, they arrived in the post! The best annual dividend so far has been thirty-two pence so money well spent! I would commend my old employer to anyone, they are fantastic!*

*Now I think about things long and hard sometimes, when my back is bellowing in the night. I think genetically the chain has broken a few generations back.*

*The natural selection process used to weed out the numpties and those with a death wish, but I have clear and unequivocal evidence that the gene pool is broken. I don't watch gameshows, as I was banned years ago for getting the answers right 100%, clearly unbeknown to the management who was preparing supper, that we viewing on plus one! I had seen it an hour before and memorised the answers.*

*Anyhow I digress, I watched The Chase last night and one individual really challenged the envelope of common sense. A lady who lives in Surrey, was asked where Peppa Pig world was in the UK? She retorted it* was in Hampshire on the way to the Lake District! The host almost had an involuntary leak! Then she said it was almost in the Lake District as she had been there several times!!!!

I have driven by it many times over the years when I used to that thing called 'work'. it's in Poulton's Park just off the M27 close to the New Forest. I have concluded as a species we are finished!

Day 18.

A very chilled day to the point where I was awake for hours in the night. The moon setting at the end of the garden was worthy of a photo, but camera battery was flat and I couldn't find the charger in the dark.

We haven't needed anything up to this point but it seems we only have eight days of cat food left. Looking at the big boys there are no delivery slots for weeks but one of the small guys can send it by Saturday for the same price as the supermarkets.

Looking at the news it's clear that all over the country parents are unable to control their children, they do what they want. Our local council has a skate park in Whitstable, still full of yobs, the council send a team there every day consisting of two policemen and a council enforcement officer, and still, they keep going!

Maybe it's another way of displaying the natural selection process? I think it's appalling, these officers could and should, be doing real policing not what moron parents should be doing as a natural thing!

The self-isolation thing is definitely working around here, very proud of my neighbours and fellow villagers. One of the cars hasn't turned a wheel for nineteen days, so going to stick a trickle charge on the old girl today!

We should have been halfway through a break to the lake district this week, hopefully the floods of visitors have kept away to protect the locals.

I have a seed of an idea running around my head for a new book. I am in possession of all my grandfather's letters to his son who was killed in Crete 1941 and vickverky! More thought needed and finish the current one first!

Might have a day off today, I deserve it!

Day 19.

The day off was very relaxing with little to report other than I have written quite a bit today. So, treat this like a holiday in the Caribbean, sitting on the patio by the pool with copious amounts of beer and wine whilst reading a book or three. So, after watching the clear blue-sky cloud over, the pool aka small puddle on patio has dried up we are left with few options.

Beer all gone days ago, wine on route via Waitrose delivery van (two hours late at least). I think those guys deserve a medal for the crap they have to put up with from the great unwashed. I do however recommend a superb drink, one-part rum, one scrape of nutmeg, a pinch of ginger, a drip of Angostura bitters and two parts Lucozade! That's the best drink ever!

Hens wouldn't go away last night, every time I opened the back door to slide their hatch shut, they came out like parachutists on a night exercise. The quieter I crept up on them the more animated their launch became.

*I did take exception to this and it was gone 10pm, before they finally crashed out.*

*What is it with hens? Why do they think they own the joint? On the last couple of escapes, they were wearing capes and head torches!*

*On a more intriguing note, I have my first book on Kindle worldwide, up to this point I have only made sales (£1.99 each a real bargain – see couldn't help myself!) in the English-speaking countries which I am humbled by, I mean why would anyone want to read it after all? So, I had a look at the sales graph a little while ago and I see I have sold one in India!!! Why would anyone buy such a book there! It's in English as well. Oh well, back to my cup of tea and invisible chocolate brownie!*

Day 20.

*Crikey, has it been twenty days since we self-isolated? It seems like years! We are ok for supplies still, with beer and wine incoming via a nice man in a van! I have gently caressed the last remaining tin of Plumrose bacon grille!*

*If you close your eyes and sniff the tin, you can replay the smell and taste from the memory banks from a time somewhere in a wet wood in West Germany! Supper tonight will be bacon grille, eggs and beans. Later on, probably the spare bed for me!*

*Looking at the weather forecast and direction of the wind on Sunday I would not be surprised if we don't see a swallow or a house martin around from then.*

*I think today will be spent tidying the office, I have a few things I have mislaid over the last few years. I have* a battery charger, wallet and loads of important paperwork including the cat microchip certificates to find.

While I mention the cats, this was the early morning alarm today. One of them, Sampson is seven now, but he is known as the eternal kitten. He acts like a three-month-old kitten. He has many friends in his head and they come around to play with him all the time, they get up to all sort of things. Today at 5am we were playing chase the wildebeest along the landing, this time he also managed to round up a few more of the real cats to help.

The thundering sounded like the neighbours trundling the bins down the path in a synchronised fashion whilst tap dancing. The vision this conjures up doesn't bear thinking about.

Anyhow, because Sampson had real friends today for a change, he was trilling at the top of his voice which together with the thundering brought us awake to start the daily grind two hours early. Another day in paradise…

Whilst making the third or fourth cup of tea I was idly looking out the window. On the beam extension about eighteen inches from the glass is a bag of bird nuts, I haven't seen a bird there for ages and today my luck changed.

There were tit's all over my nut bag and it was wobbling about quite excitedly! The last time it moved like that it had a starling trying to steal it.

I might plant a few courgettes and tomatoes today in preparation for the long haul, I will pick up a few pots from the garage while I restock the nuts from the big bin.

Day 21.

*Oh dear, I seem to have caused a bit of inuendo A young lady I have known for well over thirty years, has pointed out that the container for the bird food and the said birds feeding on them, may have been taken as a little risqué. Completely unintentional I assure you.*

*We have had a very entertaining afternoon watching the next-door neighbour get his fix of golf. He usually plays six days a week except for shopping day, but he uses this free time wisely to polish his bats and remove the mud from his electric cart.*

*Well today he has set up a driving range in his garden. A blanket has been suspended between our fences and a small net at the end of the garden about four feet high. He has his pin things on the patio and he whacks the balls hard into the blanket.*

*On the face of it nothing wrong with this, but he keeps missing the blanket and sends his balls way down the field. The sheep had to run just now as a bright green ball whisked passed the fat one's ear!*

*Not content with missing once, he did it over and over again, until he was 'without balls. He then couldn't get into the field to retrieve them as it was padlocked. He can't climb the gate so the field is full of green balls!*

The nearest I came to playing golf was when the Sandwich Open tournament was in full flow. When I lived there, I was issued with a 'LR' sticker (local resident) or local retards as suggested by some of the ruder golf nuts!

The funniest thing about today's events was he was dressed to play, plus fours, brogues, pringle jumper and a check cap at a jaunty angle!

I may get my fly fishing gear out tomorrow and practise casting down the field, it's always best to keep up the practise you never know when a trout will pass by.

Now here is a conundrum, my rod licence expired on the 31$^{st}$ March so technically I am 'fishing' outside the law. Will they send round a panda car if they see me?

I planted the courgettes and tomatoes but now out of potting compost. I am going to sneak out in the field tonight, to snaffle the tops off molehills, so I can get some cucumbers and salad planted. I am also going to plant beans in the plant pots in the front garden, and potatoes in the lawn, the neighbours will be talking about me again!

Day 22.

I now have a plan for fishing, thanks Neil, will be in touch when we are safe to go out. I will have to plan a trip to the dog food shop soon, only have nineteen days of dog food in stock, after that Rigsby might be hungry! Perhaps an early morning trip to Pets are Robbers before it gets busy midweek?

We have reorganised the freezers to make stock control easier, today we have a roast beef supper. The beef from 2016 has defrosted well and doesn't smell *(other than of beef!) so horseradish at the ready. I'm coming for you!*

*We virtually returned from the lake district yesterday, a long and tiring journey usually six hours, but did it from the comfort of the sofa in about twelve seconds. Nice to see the road works on the M6 have finished for a while. Whilst unpacking and washing the virtual clothes, we realised that the big suitcase with the Caribbean stickers on needs to be brought into action.*

*We fly to St Lucia on the thirteenth from Gatwick on a virtual BA flight. Virtual beer and wine with virtual top-class food at the best resort in the Leeward Islands, Sandals Halcyon look it up on google earth!*

*More gentle gardening today, back is playing up so the garden chairs should get a bash later, might even put up the umbrella! Stay safe!*

Day 23.

*Well one swallow doesn't make a summer but we all need something to hang our hats on at the moment. Yes, a swallow drifted by and it's was warm and dry yesterday so yes in my book it's summer! Dodgy shirt and the obligatory shorts time again!*

*As we are now at home for the foreseeable future, I have been planting veg which normally dries out, as we are away a few times during the early summer. I can't wait for the shoots to emerge (Seeds dated 2012!) hopefully!*

*It's been so quiet over the last few days; Stone street is a mile away and there is always a hum and buzz from passing vehicles, but this has diminished to the occasional truck passing down to Folkestone. My car has only moved a few yards for three weeks now. It needs fuel so will try and pop to garage later today, Morrison's fuel is now only just over a pound per litre, but nowhere to drive to.*

*Starting to tidy the garage today, you can barely get down to the back wall, but I have no idea what's really stored there so today is the day! Inside jobs today as it is going to rain!*

Day 24.

*Ordered dog food this a monthly recurring delivery, so the boy won't have to eat my arm if this goes on much longer.*

*I did order some coffee but the expected delivery date came through as seventh of May! I was getting twitchy so Sue found some on Viking direct so Wednesday it is... Until an email came saying the original arrives today! By Wednesday I will be in possession of six kilos of Italian coffee! The maths again suggest two cups per day, equals four months of coffee!*

*Tiger Woods was at it again today this time with a different pringle jumper and blue brogues! His balls had turned pink and he then proceeded to do a rerun of the chaos of a few days ago! I was intrigued, so I pulled up a chair and watched intently.*

*Many years ago, we had a firing range in the army called the moving target range where we would blast away the taxpayer's money, trying to hit a cardboard man running backwards and forwards. I visualise the scene of all those years ago but here we were, Tiger blatting pink balls down the range with the very fed up black sheep running backwards and forwards trying not to get hit.*

*Incidentally as an aside, the green balls were still where they fell from the previous attempt. I called over the fence during a lull asking if he wanted sheep for supper but Tiger only grunted!*

*Is it a correlation between natives of his country of birth (North Wales) and sheep? I firmly believe he is certain they should run in circles (Due to legs on one side of the animals' body being shorter) to enable the sheep to remain upright, when walking round the mountainside in its natural habitat. I guess this gene has been bred out on lowland sheep over the generations, making all legs equal length!*

*I can't get the vision of the moving target range, with a sheep strapped to the target pole out of my head!*

Day 25.

*I have a serious message before I move to the daily humdrum. For those who don't know I work with military veterans who struggle with their mental health, signposting them to the various support services, together with the older veterans who live on their own and get a bit lonely and isolated. I tend to do 90% of this through facebook/facebook messenger.*

*Many of my friends send me jokes, support for charities, NHS rainbows, plus all the other good stuff for morale etc, can you please all do me a favour please? I missed an important message yesterday because it was lost in the huge mass of the daily fun stuff. Would all my friends please miss me out of the jokes and support messages until this crisis subsides a bit? I do really appreciate them and support wholeheartedly all the good work going on, can you leave my message box alone for a while please. I don't want to miss any more veterans in need of a bit of help!*

*OK so down to the important stuff, getting a bit tired of long-life milk now, it does have a strange taste but can't bring myself to drink tea or coffee without the white stuff! I have tried lemon and cinnamon but it's a bit yukky!*

*We haven't been out now for twenty-five days, and will try to stay in until we really need to venture to the shops. Still no delivery slots available!*

*Tiger changed tack yesterday, he has a fine silver birch tree which overhangs our garden a little. We have been concerned with the amount of ivy going up the tree.*

*The ivy is over an inch in circumference and almost to the top of the tree. Tiger was out there tapping away at the vines with a bolster chisel and a wooden mallet.*

*This took all day to remove the vines, tapping like a rampant woodpecker echoed across the field and around the houses. Fortunately, this stopped the golf ball sheep chasing so I am sure they appreciated a day off!*

Day 26 and 27.

*Well, it's been a challenging couple of days, although I back up my laptop frequently, I hadn't done it for a couple of days. Guess what? I had written about six pages of A4 on the new book so wasn't best pleased! I was sweating a bit I can assure you, but all became clear once I plugged my test meter in, the power cable wasn't giving any voltage.*

*Remember a few days ago I mentioned the sofa was pulled out? Well, that's the problem, the sofa ended up on the power lead (low voltage side) and broke the cable.*

*I have cut that two inches out, taped it up, rerouted it and we are back in business. I have just backed up and will again every time I touch the book!*

*Until yesterday I had hands like an office worker, all the callouses cuts and dry skin of the motor trade had long gone, (except for the blunt fingertips from too much typing lately!) I will explain further on!*

*Tiger decided he wanted to remove a small tree in his garden, I didn't offer as I can't bend down at the moment, back is killing me from falling over the broom, so no chance matey. After a quick brief on the 100% reliable Bennett chainsaw, I pulled it and it went first time as usual and handed it over.*

*Tiger's boss called 'Lunch' and he was gone like a long dog over the hill!*

*About thirty-one and a half minutes later, he was back on the job whilst I prepared the score cards from the comfort of my patio chair. He pulled and pulled whilst puffing and panting. After about five minutes I asked if he had turned on the power switch? No, he hadn't and by now it had flooded so it wouldn't start!*

*Another thirty minutes passed, and eventually it fired up in a huge cloud of white smoke. three Seconds later it stopped as he jammed it into his tree, and the ornamental bricks at the base! The chain flew off and looped.*

*I then spend fifteen minutes stripping down the gears, and flattening out the chain! I, have never seen such a knot in the chain in all the years of owning and using one. So, all working again it took about two seconds to remove the small bush, which on inspection a bow saw would have done as well but in less time!*

*My hands are now engrained in chainsaw oil, cuts and scrapes. I could have been back to 1978, changing a clutch on a Matra Bagheera with all the angst and filth that brought with it.*

*Mental note to self, when Tiger asks to borrow anything again suggest it's been pinched from the garden by the pikeys! I have just backed up again!*

Day 28,

*We gave ourselves a day off today, sitting in my Caribbean shirt with my St Lucia hat on this fine day. On the thirteenth of this month, we would have been travelling on a helicopter to our favourite resort on the lovely island of St Lucia. Had a look at next year and it's double dear so far. Will keep checking I need a deal!*

*All the neighbours seem to be fiddling around in their front gardens just to get to speak to each other, even six feet apart is too close in my book!*

*Supper was interesting today, a four-year-old lamb joint from the freezer dated 2016, a swede and a parsnip both bought just before Christmas, and roast* potatoes from the bag of spuds bought at the end of January! Yum!

I inherited my parents' tabletop mincer; it was used every week until 2012 from 1952 and there is a date embossed on it of 1951.

Today it's clamped to the kitchen worktop to hand grind lamb into mince for onward conversion to a shepherd's pie for supper!

Getting the hang of this 1950s living now, been knocking up a few ration coupons to be included in our monopoly set for added authenticity, during these interesting times.

Pressure washer coming out later to be stripped down and leak repaired, the patio is a bit green from the lack of sunlight, needs a blast off (Ok might not do it today as there is a need to pace myself!)

Day 29,

The routine around here is pretty much the same every day now, the neighbours come out in their front garden around late morning just as an excuse to yell at each other across the gardens, normally they hate each other but now they do it with a smile.

I suppose its human nature as pack animals to feel the need to communicate with each other. Some people don't do too well on their own without outside contact.

We are fine here; the hens and cats had a sing song last night and Rigsby the dog provided the deep bass notes. It went well until the last few notes of 'we are the champions' when Rigs gentle bass tone turned into a howl as he went far above his normal voice range! Painful! The sound of windows closing was in perfect unison.

*Around about this time we would have been driving to the hotel in preparation for the trip abroad.*

*Time to look at some photos today, I think. The sky is as blue as the Caribbean today, there seems less pollution around I could sit in a chair in the garden and remember just how good it is, but it's not warm enough yet!*

Day 30.

*Grumpy codger day today, as I write I should be sitting in seat 44J on flight BA 2154 heading to a faraway place, but that's not made me grumpy... much! What has made me grumpy is looking at the TV and papers, watching all the youngsters basically doing what they like.*

*We have been home for thirty days now, no shop trips, no farm shops, no trip to Folkestone to ride home a lobster etc. The people of my age had parents who at huge personal sacrifice, gave us all the world we have today.*

*These idiots without thinking will make sure the remaining members of that brave generation, get knocked off way before their time! This is not right, £10k fines plus four days in the stocks for eggs to be thrown (ps I have more eggs than I can eat!) I have also noticed that Greta Thumper has been conspicuous by her absence from the media recently, I wonder why?*

*I have also found out that DHL have dropped my case of beer! Although the company, (Greene King) have instantly agreed to replace it, I am now down to a single St Omer stubby from 1982, found at the back of the cupboard to last three or four days!*

*We have been loyal to one supermarket for years but still can't get a delivery slot from them! We will change loyalties when we go back to normal!*

*I think everyone will look at what they do different after this has calmed down! (Mrs B can now make a whole courgette last for a stir fry, casserole, ratatouille and still have some left over to give to the hens!)*

Day 31

*Another fun-packed day in paradise, Caribbean corn beef hash for breakfast with sauté potatoes. Neatly cubed Fray Bentos lightly fried corned beef, onions chunked, red pepper and the magic ingredient a scotch bonnet chilli! Washed down with ice cold orange juice to put out the fire!!*

*Sitting in the lounge randomly gazing into space it's amazing how the imagination plays tricks on you. The wall above the watercolour of the Kentish Oast appeared to bulge and swell, after much eye rubbing and summoning the long haired (much longer now due to missed hair appointment) general, it was concluded that indeed there was a huge bulge appearing.*

*Being a bloke, I poked it to see what would happen (well you would wouldn't you!) and it burst, sending a shower of water everywhere.*

*The cistern in the bathroom had jammed and the flow of water in exceeded the water going out of the overflow. You can now see why this wasn't written yesterday, as some serious plumbing and removing of bathroom fittings, to resolve the leak! Valve stripped down, crud removed, wobbly bit realigned and finally supervising the water clean-up, and drying out process.*

Day 32.

*Catching up with the narrative today, following yesterday's day of work (I didn't think that would happen again!) I decided to reward myself with a good day off!*

*Concurrently the chicken in the fridge was deemed ready to cook as it was on its date. A roast dinner came into plan and I settled back with the knowledge it would be rather tasty!*

*I am concerned that the management are taking this lock in too seriously, that nagging Alexa lady keeps telling me there is someone at your door. Firstly, a guy turns up with a huge box of bread mix packets, enough for a loaf a week until Christmas, thirty minutes later, another driver from DPD (the ring the bell and run-away company!) this time it was long life milk, twenty packs@ two litres a pop. I like my porridge but it's getting silly now.*

*So, the external interest began around 11am, Tiger appeared on the path outside complete with hose, power lead, pressure washer and golf cart thingy. This was starting to look interesting so we settled down in the kitchen window with a brew and watched. After about ten minutes the cart thingy was replaced with his car.*

*A plan was hatched, we would have a race! It would pass the time and when bets were laid, the person who does the washing up would be decided! Obviously, our industrious neighbour was bored, he never cleans his car, the nice man from Lithuania does it in the golf club car park for a fiver a pop! I would referee!*

*We agreed when the doors came open the oven would go on and the roast chicken race was on! Behind me furious vegetable preparation was under way, outside the floor mats came out together with golf bats, and assorted peaked baseball caps with all the 'logos' scattered along the pavement. The doors were then shut and the car was pressure washed.*

*The water went all over the mats and the other detritus scattered about. Meanwhile the chicken had been wrestled to the ground, stuffed, and inserted firmly into the oven on a trivet of veg and fresh sage, thyme and rosemary from the garden. The veg was blanched, roast potatoes laid out ready to go.*

*Returning to the other competitor, he was hoovering his wet mats on the pavement and doing the footwells on the car. The mats were reinstated but he hadn't looked underneath them as the dust, road muck etc, was placed into the clean footwell under the mats. I deducted a point for this schoolboy error!*

*The car was washed by hand, taking care to do the alloy wheels first and then the glass and body (same water of course!) The windows were polished inside and out, in my book a bit half-heartedly to be fair, the smears were then obvious where they were clear before he started. behind me the bird was resting, potatoes in oven and veg ready to go. Gravy was finished and I blew the whistle. Bennett 1, Tiger 0, I can't wait for next week's rematch!*

*Chicken consumed at a leisurely pace and whilst cleaning up I noticed Tiger was wiping his engine and the bay. This astounded me as I didn't think he knew where the bonnet release was?*

Day 33.

 Before I start, I wish to offer an apology for what I about to write, a newcomer to my blog would say that I have made it all up, this would apply in spades today because what I witnessed, you wouldn't see on a TV gameshow, or indeed make it up!

 Today started well, the hens behaved and despite the over use of beak stick they delivered the goods as usual. The two bantams are laying now so we get a dozen a day. I refused to enter into negotiations over a price, I reminded them I provide the food and clean them out twice a week! They may sulk tomorrow but I don't care!

 Breakfast was a treat, I came downstairs to a jug of pancake batter, this disappeared quickly and the last one I am very proud of! I made a spiny anteater shape in the pan which went down well!

 So, the big story of the day started well, Tiger next door was wandering aimlessly round the garden this morning so exchanged pleasantries and I carried on with my hen polishing etc. I looked up a few minutes later it had started!

 As a bit of background, we live in a close that's been built to look like a group of Kentish barns over three storeys, all the same. We have covenants so we can't park caravans, change the colour or put up Sky dishes etc etc.

Most have their dishes at the very bottom of their back gardens at knee level, out of sight of the covenant police. Here was the golfmeister, tin of pledge furniture polish in hand, polishing his Sky dish! I called over and advised him that it wouldn't make the screen on his TV clearer, he should clean his glasses instead. He didn't take too kindly to that and went indoors.

Clearly this guy is bored and suffering from golf withdrawal. About thirty minutes later he comes down the garden with a stepladder and proceeded to wash the inside windows of his conservatory. I am convinced he was using the same cloth he cleaned the alloy wheels with previously. Our conservatories are up against the borders, so we have six inches between the buildings and with the doors open every word can be heard.

His management came in and pointed out just how smeary and dirty they now were. He was sent off whilst they were done again with some vigour (I think the management was busy and didn't have inplan a window cleaning exercise today).

Tiger appeared again with a long pole and the hose reel. We took up position on the patio and awaited developments armed with a cup of coffee and a small snack!

The hose was pulled out and connected he then went through the conservatory pulling the hose behind him, the look on the face of his management committee was a picture, she looked over at us raised her eyebrows and shrugged her shoulders!

Their bedroom window was opened, and the hose hung out over the lip of the Velux frame. He came back and collected the long pole. On inspection it was a very long spray bar, probably eight feet long. He had turned the hose on and then plugged the bar into the connecter.

As everyone knows if you turn the tap on, pressure build up and when you 'break the seal' water sprays everywhere until it clicks in. On cue, water shot out all over him and his bedroom and probably seeped back down the hose to pool on the carpet below the window.

The conservatory roof windows were sprayed and the dust that had gathered over the recent dry weather was moved around a bit. Now the roof was smeared and muddy. Silence prevailed for some hours next door!

Day 34.

I can't believe how other people lead such interesting lives; we blunder from one day to the next without too much excitement.

Our neighbours however are really on the ball. Tiger was out there again smacking balls into his blanket and beyond, I was reading my book and didn't really take much notice, the thump of the ball into the blanket and the 'smack' of the bat and the silence indicating he had missed, carried on for a while. He then said to Mrs Tiger 'Can you tie me up again?' I was up out of my chair like a long dog and peering through the fence like Nora Batty.

Tiger had a length of washing line around the tops of his arms, Mrs Tiger obviously hadn't knotted it properly and the master of the house was requiring further tying up. The rope was duly redone with it tight *half way up his upper arms, and he proceeded to smack balls again.*

*I couldn't help myself, I had to ask the question, 'Do you have a strange perversion or is there a logical reason for the activity? Somewhat grumpily, he exclaimed I am 'Chicken Legging'! I didn't ask, I had to go indoors for a lie down! Any golfers have any ideas?*

*I am an expert in 'Ferret Legging' having held the record for putting two ferrets down my trousers back in 1976, but other than that... no idea! I think it's a secret game that went badly wrong, Mrs Tiger getting her revenge for the window cleaning saga!*

*The smell indoors was getting better and better, homemade bread was baking and concurrently eggs were boiling. Scotch eggs were on the cards and fresh baked bread. A picnic in the garden tomorrow I feel. I have to applaud the management; bread isn't easy to do by hand so what a fantastic treat! I though, have failed miserably,*

*I tried to put my flag up in the front garden to celebrate a certain regimental battle honour but the hole seems to have moved. I finally found it poking around with a stick, much to the amusement of the gradually growing crowd of neighbours, so the flag flies tall and proud! A glass of port to toast I feel!*

Day 35.

*Wowsers this bread is the mutts! I haven't had bread like this in years! More on order! It will defeat all the good work I have done with my diet earlier in the year (I say that because last time I looked up it was January!)*

*One of the bantams has gone broody now, only had two days of both laying, just back to one now! Little bit ticked today; I had a comment yesterday to the effect of 'why are you sitting around all day when you could be helping the effort with voluntary work??' Well just for clarity, we are self-isolating because Sue has a delicate chest and is prone to asthma, so hence why we are at home.*

*I have not been sitting around all day, I have been bidding for funding to get the museum website revamped with some success, in addition to that I spend about three to four hours a day working with veterans' welfare, so yes, I am at home but working hard to support others!*

*Moan over, Tiger has burnt himself out, not seen him today at all. So, peace prevails around the close. The beer finally arrived after DHL dropped the first shipment, twelve bottles = twenty-four days' worth of beer unless a pint glass accidently finds itself at the front of the cupboard!*

*Rigsby has been a bit unwell most evenings, the smell has been unbelievable, his food hasn't changed so we were considering a trip to the vet, an outing not to be taken lightly! But he was caught yesterday with his eight-foot-long licker, removing bantam poo deftly from their crate! Anyone wants a minging Labrador with some minor bad habits!*

Day 36.

*I can't believe we have not had contact with anyone nor been out in the car for thirty-six days. Car batteries to go on trickle charge when the weather returns to sunshine! Thanks to Robin Smith for the dog food link, the 'Guffador' should be sorted now.*

Day 37.

*After spending a while sorting my new beers into colour/strength order, I decided to give myself a day off today, we have a WIFI booster so I was sitting on the patio reading the Daily Snail on my tablet, when I thought I heard someone talking in a non-native tone, I ignored it but it became louder and more familiar.*

*I looked down the garden and realised it was Tiger, he was extremely cross and very red in the face. I would point out here that he comes from the Land of the Dragon, not far in fact from my MIL somewhere near Ruthin, hence the familiarity in the cursing and swearing.*

*Unbeknown to either of them in the past I have run this through Google translate (voice recognition) and believe me those Welsh guys know how to swear! My MIL should know better at her age!*

*I digress, Tiger was calling to Mrs Tiger who obviously couldn't hear him as she was on the front doorstep nattering to one of the neighbours. He was standing a little strangely, he had a plastic 'thingy' in one hand whilst holding the gate latch with the other. When I enquired whether he was ok he replied that he had been repairing his 'thingy' with superglue and the tube split sticking him firmly to the 'thingy', this was now made* worse when he tried to get back into his garden from the scene of the disaster.

He had grabbed the latch on the gate and superglued himself to that as well!

I mentioned to Mrs Tiger that he needed help whilst keeping a respectable distance. The cursing carried on for a bit until the Stanley knife blade was found and eventually all went quiet. No golf today I feel!

Day 38.

Although we were pretty stocked up with food and essentials. (I have been threatening to dump the freezer in the office for three years but not quite got round to it) The freezer has now some big holes in its storage space.

We decided to try and get a shopping delivery, all the big boys no chance, if you haven't use them before hard luck! We don't like to shop online normally, why would we? We are retired, we supposedly have more time on our hands... yeah right!

Anyhow I digress, the Guffador woke up at midnight and demanded a quick exit. He then barked loudly and wouldn't shut up. In the end I had to go down the garden and advise him that my slightly well-loved slippers with the toe hanging out, would soon be connecting with his bum if he didn't shut up!

That did it, but when I turned around the houses that were in complete darkness, now have all the bedroom lights blaring down the gardens. None of us have curtains at the rear of the house, the nearest human habitation is a mile at least, so no real need! If comments are passed, I will tell them he was seeing off the sheep rustlers!

On return I decided to have a cup of tea as I was as wide awake as most of my neighbours. I checked the Morrison's site and there was a slot! OK it's in three weeks but I am in! Item one. Doombar, Item two Wine and so on.

Happy days, I returned to my pit of slumber to find the Guffador had decided to take up my spot, and was lying on my pillow upside down. Rather than wake the house again I slunk off to the spare bed, turfed off six cats and crashed out!

A difficult choice this morning, as I was on my own should I do a full breakfast including the mushrooms and black pudding (Sue doesn't eat breakfast that often!) or should I get points? So, after a few milliseconds a points increase was on the cards.

The last of the home cooked bread was placed in the toaster, two eggs were boiled for about two and a half minutes (Alexa does my timing normally but today she was flashing bright red so I didn't pursue that route!) Best guessed and presented the breakfast and confirmed points total!

More bread on the cards today! In the depths of the freezer appears to be a complete turkey and Shergar, we must rotate the contents more often!

Day 39.

Busy day all round, Sue created the most marvellous casserole, which left me lying face down slurping like a demented swine hog! Two more meals to go, dumplings tonight and pie crust tomorrow! I have been working, well I say that loosely, more like working *on the book of my childhood memories. I have a cost for printing it, just need to work out how to get it paid for!*

*The intention is to have the costs paid so all the book sales can be divided between the churches in the villages where I lived as a child.*

*I throw this into the ring for comments, how do I raise 2k? facebook fundraiser? Crowdfunding (whatever that is)? Or blatant asking people for money but not keen on that option really. Any local businesses wanting to support this out there?*

*As I write this, I would just be getting off the flight from St Lucia, having had a fitful night's sleep and steeling myself for the M25, a journey done so many times for work, but now I detest with a passion.*

*I always find Gatwick a game of two halves, travellers arriving to go on a flight to a faraway place always have a smile and sense of optimism, travellers returning always look miserable and fed up. This to me seems the wrong way round, surely you are refreshed and up for new challenges when you get back from your annual Hollier's?*

Day 40.

*Weird behaviour around here seems to be spreading, perhaps it's me? I have to say I did play a blinder on next door a couple of years ago. When I moved in there was a whitethorn hedge between us but it was eight feet high. I kept cutting it but it was a real effort. In the middle of the stems was the original fence which represents the boundary.*

*On the plan the 'T' is definitely on the other side so I approached Tiger, to see if he minded me removing it and putting a more solid fence just inside the boundary. Tiger was happy with that and it happened.*

*About six months later the other neighbour asked if he could renew the fence his side, I agreed, it was falling down and covered in various shrubs long overrun etc.*

*This was my boundary which I pointed out that I was going to do the fence at some point. He couldn't wait so did it anyway!*

*So back to the beginning, Tiger has forgotten that the boundary between us is his, and the other neighbour his side has a very low fence on the boundary. The problem with this is that 'CatMan' owns the boundary (I will explain CatMan in a while) Tiger wants to put up a* five-foot fence, as cat man is always chatting to him over the fence which annoys Tiger. If he had a five-foot fence, Tiger could sit on his patio in his pants!

CatMan happened to ask if I had a ground plan and I indicated affirmative, when asked who owned what, I did tell a minute porky. CatMan and Tiger well at it across the fence just now, Tiger wants a fence, cat man payed for it to be renewed ten years ago and didn't want a barrier! Hilarious, I will deny any knowledge and sit back and watch the sparks fly!

Now CatMan, he detests cats, and hates it when ours wander by, in total there are twenty-seven cats within a short radius, OK we have seven but five don't get out of bed, and the other two certainly don't go near his garden!

To stop the cats, CatMan has put chicken wire up his fence at the back of the properties, and nailed a neat strip of chicken wire along the top of the gate. This provides a perfect scratching post and they all queued up waiting for a turn!

When he realised this was happening, he invented the best cat deterrent I have ever seen, He nailed coir doormat to the top of the gate, and vertically on the frame of the gate. Perfect for scratching, not only do they queue but they have synchronised scratching competitions. three on the top at once and another scoring whilst the remaining audience look on!

The 'who owns what' argument continues, Tiger is out there with a clipboard and binoculars trying to work out who owns which broken or cracked tile on the roof.

To close the day of fun, clearly Mrs Tiger has mediated and banged their heads together! They are now *both ripping out the adjoining fence between them which has unearthed a vast quantity of broken bricks.*

*Now I champion teamwork and a fine example has been shown here. Tiger has his wheelbarrow on the back path, he then proceeds to climb the fence into the back paddock (brave man I say, the owner is a feared individual!) A five-foot ranch fence was climbed at some personal cost. Tiger is past seventy and vertically challenged. This took seven minutes to complete, CatMan passed the wheelbarrow over, and then proceeded to carry broken bricks one at a time, to the waiting transport.*

*Now the combined age of these combatants is well over one hundred and fifty, and the carrying took an age. Tiger, using his best camouflage skills learnt in the RMP an eon ago proceeded to push the wheel barrow right across the middle of the paddock. Brave man because if he had encountered the owner of the paddock he would have been lacerated by the vengeful tongue. The bricks were then thrown into the field beyond. This was repeated many times until I became bored.*

*A little while later the farmer appears and looking confused collects up the bricks and throws them back into the paddock. I am staying up all night to await the impending fireworks!*

*It's a good job I have some beer chilled!*

Day 41.

*I was up early today, bit of a short night, Vengeful woman was out in her paddock for hours last night, wearing a head torch. The bricks are neatly stacked at the end of her field and the green and orange golf balls have now been placed at the end of Tigers path, neatly spelling out a very rude word in alternate coloured balls, sadly Tiger collected them up before I could photograph them (not that I could post as it was a very, very rude word!)*

*A good day yesterday, some serious sport had at the expense of everyone around. It's very unusual here at the moment. The weather is fantastic, the air quality is superb and the sky is so blue. It reminds me of being a child growing up in the countryside when I was seven or eight.*

*The noise is minimal, both air traffic and road noise barely audible above the bird song. You can hear skylarks in the back field now, they were always masked by road noise. I don't think we will see this again in my lifetime.*

*Over the last three years the bees have been scarce, this year they are everywhere, again air pollution and traffic may play a part. Even the air smells differently, only those of a certain age would remember! Maybe perhaps just maybe we have been given a chance to remind ourselves just how smart a world we live in!*

*As I sit on the patio reminiscing like an old duffer, the doorbell went. A small man with a white van delivered a parcel for which I had to smile nicely into his camera (scary prospect with a four-week beard and hair now long enough to plait!) It was for Sue, excitedly she ripped the packaging apart and there it was, ten kilograms of pizza dough flour!! So, I have reserved an entire cupboard in the office for the latest arrival and sit here patiently for Sue, aka 'Domino' to test the mix out!*

*Domino was just getting the scales ready and another delivery arrived, in the words of the current ad on the TV 'Ooh I wonder what that can be?' no not bloody gin, 2000 tea bags and another five packs of bloody bread dough!*

*It's tough being retired, the old income isn't what it was back in the day. I had a thought yesterday, no one has started their cars for over five weeks so some serious flat batteries will be around in the near future. I made up a sign and placed it at the end of the close 'Jump Starts £5 a go!' with my phone number.*

*I have a spare battery fully charged by the portable solar panel, so into the wheelbarrow it went along with the industrial jump leads once belonging to Canterbury Motor Co. Not long to wait, I did six in five minutes, the nosiness of people looked at the sign and went straight for their car keys, followed closely by their phones!*

*I saw Tiger earlier, he as usual took the mickey out of the power leads leading to Domino's SLK (Which only does two hundred miles a year I might add). I was topping up the battery with the charger! He scoffs and derides the lack of use etc (It's a 1998 and done less than twenty thousand miles!) Yes, it needs its battery charged sometimes as it doesn't get the use.*

*I explained all cars would lose a certain degree of charge not moving for five weeks. He scoffed and chuntered and wandered off. Whilst putting away the charger I noted his interior light was on! Oh, it's so sweet! Revenge that is! I will charge him fifty quid when he grovels and asks nicely for a jump!*

Day 42.

*I am the top dog around here, the man with the power! Sadly, my back has given up so I have to pay one* of the local lads to hump the wheelbarrow, my net profit has reduced to £1 a jump, otherwise he will stay in bed! Such is the youth of today.

Now I have a conspiracy theory for you all to consider. There was a string of white lights in the sky last night, fortunately I had read earlier that they were a string of satellites.

Now this is very 'War of the Worlds' stuff. Now here is the thought provoker. The architect of the satellite program is Elon Musk the American billionaire who leads the way in battery car technology. OR is he? Is he not the advance party from a faraway alien world, sent to lull us into a false sense of security?

The aliens will come and we will not notice, they will steal all our sweeties and then we will be in serious trouble mark my words!

I certainly need a haircut now, it's almost long enough to put up in a bun! (Angela Pridham feel free to post that photo of us from 1976!) Domino was chasing me around with the plastic bowl and the pink kitchen scissors earlier, but I resisted the temptation to allow her access.

This seems ungrateful you ask, but believe me this is entirely sensible. About four years ago I had a large black hair sticking out of the top my nose, every time I looked down my nose it looked like a unicorn horn! I asked Domino to pluck it out for me, so armed with tweezers and a torch the operation began! It wouldn't come out and, in the end, a random grasp pulled it from its sleepy hollow, together with a big chunk of skin.

I had a plaster on my nose for days as it would not stop bleeding. This is why I am reluctant to have my hair trimmed, I could lose the top of my ears or worse!

*I have to admit that I am in big trouble today, we have a variegated bush just outside our kitchen window, in the mornings the sun shines through there, but at the moment it's a little dark because of the bush.*

*Without consultation or a letter of instruction, I decided to cut it down to improve the view so we can maintain the log of comings and goings of the neighbours.*

*Domino was baking the daily loaf (incidentally one of the best, multigrain my fave!) she noticed the missing bush and went ballistic! I have had the bush cutters taken away from me, and instructed never to fiddle with her bush again.*

*I brought in the foliage I had previously dumped under next doors hedge and suggested we substitute them for the flowers that we normally have. This seemed to work and I appear to be off the hook, not sure about my points total though, will need to investigate when the time is right.*

*To close today on a note of humour, those of us who are old enough will remember the 'trim phone' back in the 1970s. When it rang it was a high-pitched repetitive note? After a while all the starlings in the village were imitating them. Dozens of trim phones ringing all at once and believe me they were very lifelike. So, it appears Tiger has a phone with a similar noise.*

*Over the last few days, he has had all his doors and windows open and of course his phone has been constantly ringing with his golf mates lamenting the lack of access.*

*Mrs Tiger was preparing supper and Tiger was in the garden beating balls into the blanket with his bats. A starling was sitting on my roof imitating the telephone down to a tee (excuse the pun!) Every time he went to swing his bat, the 'phone went off' and he trudged indoors.*

*This went on for at least fifteen minutes until the starling became bored and flew off! We of course watched this rolling around the conservatory chairs with uncontrollable laughter!*

Day 43.

*Awoke this morning to the sound of a cuckoo, first one this year! The only sound audible, no car noise from Stone Street nor farm vehicle movement around the village. It's quite eerie now. All the neighbours have adopted the holiday mode now, the close is silent until 9:00. At 9:02 I resumed the pressure washing of the lower patio, this was completed by 09:18 by then neighbours had arisen from sleepy pits to start the day refreshed, grumpy and generally miserable.*

*Revenge was achieved by them though, clearly it was bacon day and the smell wafted around for ages! We are out of bacon!*

*Tiger was about reasonably early, he had his hosepipe out which I hadn't noticed before, went through his house from the front of the building. The sight of his hose disappearing through his letter box and the visualisation of a grubby hosepipe dragged across Mrs Tiger's cream carpet was bringing a smile to my face! I didn't realise he failed in his planning to have an outside tap at the back of the house.*

*We had one built a year later complete with power and water! Anyway, he was washing white stones from the bed next to his decking, they are collected up into a small handful and placed in Mrs Tiger's kitchen colander, sprayed vigorously, then washed individually with a toothbrush. six hours later he is still doing it! The shape forming is rather good, making a nice pattern around the concrete golfer ornament!*

*The end of the day finished on a high. Domino has been cooking and baking all day (not seen any pizza yet but I sit patiently and quietly) but none of it is really for tonight. I was wandering through the local facebook group, and the answer presented itself.*

*Many years ago (well it seems like it!) there was a first-rate restaurant in Canterbury called the Bistro Vietnam, I have been there many times and the food was out of this world, Far East flavours equal or better than any high-end establishment. We are lucky to have the owners Kim and Ian living down the road.*

*Every Friday they do a takeaway service, ring it through, get a call when it's ready, social distancing and one at a time etc. FANTASTIC!*

*Now we have some vouchers we have been sitting on for a while. When we flew with a certain well-known airline owned by a beardy bloke, they rammed me with a food cart in the middle of the night and sent me flying! The 'I'm very sorry' vouchers have a date life and now we are all holidaying in our back gardens, they would expire before hell froze over.*

*I looked at the t's & c's and discovered you can use they for home delivery duty free shopping. I filled the cart with Moet, Lanson and posh gin (gin for Christmas presents), a very smart watch that talks to your phone, and various bits of jewellery.*

*I arrived at the checkout and surprise surprise! All the booze had gone! I added three battery pack chargers to the order. The vouchers and confirmation were duly dropped in the post box on the way to pick up supper from my friends down the road! This was my first venture out in the car for 43 days! I had even forgotten how to drive an automatic car!*

Day 44.

*Today has been rather odd, when we stirred the morning produced a rather strange feeling. We were up at 6am letting the hens out and feeding the menagerie.*

*There was no sound or movement around the close. By 9am nothing had changed, it was if we were sitting in the middle of a TV drama. You do hear background noise such as a car being moved, a door being shut and sometimes a bit of music drifting through the air, but not today, all very surreal.*

*We have noted during our morning dog walk that the path we use is marked with multiple wheel marks. Very good we think, people are taking the opportunity to ride their mountain bikes around the area on the footpaths before the majority of the dog walkers are about.*

*This turned out to be incorrect, a gentleman somewhat older than myself appeared over the brow of the hill with a wheelbarrow full of rotted manure. The tracks indicated that this had been done for some time, a cheery hello and off he went.*

*The manure pile is at the bottom of the valley, some one kilometre from the road. That's getting dung at a serious cost, hopefully the farmer doesn't catch him!*

By 11am the usual noise around has returned and the routine was set for the day. We of course hadn't remembered that it was Saturday, definitely a day off around here so we conceded and retired to the conservatory, and settled in to a well-earned day off.

About 4pm the peace was shattered by 'you know who' beating golf balls into his suspended blanket again.

He had obviously taken in the problem with his balls ending up in the paddock by moving to with two feet from the blanket. The power of impact was sending his balls everywhere, they were hitting him, bouncing off our fence and going into his conservatory the power of the strike was impressive for such a small guy and his persistence was commendable.

Mrs T came out eventually and asked how he intended to get the golf ball out of the conservatory gutter? He slunk off and peace returned to paradise.

A little later the hose was threaded though the letter box and stepladder was assembled. A few minutes later he had washed the ball into the downpipe and it probably now rests underground blocking the entrance to his soak away.

I suspect when it rains next week the water will back up and leak into his conservatory. We have a ten-year warranty on the conservatory so at some point there will guys in green coats crawling all over the building sadly unable to pinpoint the problem. I am not saying anything!

Sunday tomorrow, definitely a day off, it's been a very tiring week.

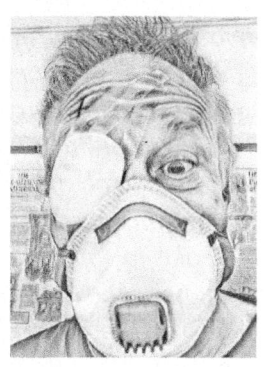

Day 45.

*There is quite a bit of negative comment about at the moment regarding the NHS, and I wanted to share my experience I had the other day to reinforce my admiration for the hard work and dedication of all the staff working so hard in this crisis.*

*A couple of days ago, I awoke in the night with a sneezing fit. I have hay fever from tree pollen and its currently in its worst stage. There was flashing lights and spots in front of my eyes. In the morning the vision in the eye was a little blurred with dark spots and a cobweb effect.*

*At 8am I called the doctors and put in the usual triage queue. With five minutes the doctor called back to arrange a face to face appointment. He asked if I could get hold of the last eye test appointment so I called my opticians. I spoke to the senior optician who was on call, he advised that I needed to be seen by an eye specialist rather than a GP, and made an immediate appointment.*

*I arrived for the appointment and within a few minutes he determined I had a torn retina and needed to see a specialist.*

Within two hours I was in Kent and Canterbury ophthalmic department. The team were fully protected with PPE and gave me a facemask. The doctor tried to laser the tear but it was right in the corner and despite best efforts, couldn't seal the tear. There was an ophthalmic surgeon finishing his list and about to go home. The team spoke to him and he agreed to operate there and then. Of course, he could have been going to the Chaucer private hospital to carry on the good work!

I duly was sorted for theatre, and the operation was completed. I was being driven home by 6pm. OK I will have to wait a couple of weeks taking it easy until they can confirm 100% success, but what a service! From Jason Gillan at Specsavers Canterbury who recognised the problem, to Mr Schultz the surgeon who stayed on to sort me out. There is no doubt in my mind without the speedy intervention, I would be looking at a long-term problem with my eyesight.

I think we have the best NHS in the world, fantastic service and thoroughly professional. If my MIL complains again that the doctor or nurse won't walk the 124 steps over the road from her surgery, (She can walk perfectly well!) I will poke my finger into her eye!

I won't be able to blog as before for at least a couple of weeks as I have virtually no vision in one eye and it's painful to focus with a serious headache, but I will be back! (dictated to the boss)


Day 49.
Feeling a lot better today, still have raging headache and vision still blurred in right eye. I would like

60

*to thank two groups of people for their messages whilst I have been AWOL. Firstly, my non-military friends for their kind messages of support and gifts left on the doorstep, with offers of free food, and secondly, my military friends for the rude abusive messages, with promises of beer that will not materialise! It amounts to the same so thanks all!*

*I had to go around to the garage yesterday to get some cat and dog food (stored in there in bulk!) and guess who I bumped into? A very grumpy Tiger! He had decided to go out and break curfew today, he went to Homebase in Folkestone to get some paint, I guess Mrs Tiger is issuing instructions and as he is still doing golf penance, he agreed willingly!*

*He stood in the queue outside in the car park which snaked around the perimeter, He must have wanted the paint very badly, imagine the grief he would have received had he returned empty handed! Anyway, after an hour he eventually arrived at the entrance to be greeted with a sign that said 'Card only', old stripy back had only gone down there without his wallet, only a wedge of cash!*

*I dashed back indoors and turned off the Alexa to hear the interesting discussion going on through our adjoining wall at some volume!*

*I think it's a habit that's ingrained from the area he comes from, my MIL is the same, she never takes her card out with her (although I am sure she is just tight!) There must have been a lot of bandits in North Wales in their youth and old habits die hard!*

*What is really amusing is that he actually admitted doing it!*

Day 50.

*Well, here we are fifty days into lockdown (OK I had to go to the hospital) but it's going very well so far. I tend to have music playing all day in the background as it helps to neutralise my tinnitus which goes from a steady hum to a fast reverse bleeper and sometimes rhythmic clicking. Today I had playing the disco classics which in a moment, transported me to a time long gone.*

*Visualise the scene, six feet two inches tall skinny bloke (waist size thirty!) whizzing along the Patrixbourne road on his 50cc moped with three gears, at twenty-nine and a half miles per hour! Dressed in the gear for the time. eight-inch heels, knee length boots. Red loons with pink flowers down the outside below the knee, grandad tie died shirt and to top that hair way down past the shoulders!*

*The riding gear consisted of the above plus a blue peanut helmet and a rather smart parka, with a rabbit fur trimmed hood complete with fleas!*

*This cool dude strutted his stuff up the steps of Bridge Country Club on a Friday night to 'get on down' to the disco beat! The night in question (and there were many!) ended in disaster.*

*Once I reached the door, I forgot that I had the Elton John boots on, recognising someone I went inside quickly and it all went black. I had forgotten I was eight inches taller than usual and cracked by head on the stone frame of the door!*

*I woke up in the ambulance having stained my tie die grandad shirt with a nice shade of red. I was too embarrassed to go back for months!*

*First day out today, we thought perhaps we could break the curfew by 'going shopping' after all we have not* been shopping for fifty-one days so in theory, we should be somewhat hungry.

We figured that if stopped by the stazi we could claim hunger had driven us from our sleepy hollow. After I all I can't drive so 'my carer' was discharging her responsibilities admirably.

We decided to drive past the meadow where we used to take the boy to burn his energy off, we stopped to look at the cowslips and we then realised 'oh dear we have left our shopping bags and wallets at home' so we took the boy for a run in his favourite meadow!

After that we had to go home but not before driving past the house of 'annual plant man' to purchase some runner bean plants! So technically we have bought food for 8 weeks' time yes, but that's fine!

Annual plant man obviously is doing his thing for community spirit this year, he is normally a robbing git, selling them for 4 quid each, this year 70p is the going rate which is just affordable when using the change from around the floor of the car! Another day in paradise!

Day 51.

Another fun day in paradise, obviously Tiger is still in trouble, he was outside beating his balls into the blanket with some vigour, grunting with each swing.

CatMan heard him and came out to discuss fences and other things garden. He was interrupting Tiger and his swing and Tiger was becoming very grumpy.

We have just had a bulk gas delivery from a new firm, our gas tank compound was installed as the same time as the houses were built back in 1987, OK you have to go down a little alley, but all tankers have enough *pipework to get there. Not my man, 'how do you get the truck down there?' He couldn't grasp the concept of parking at the end.*

*Now the clue was already in view, the opposition was parked on the' spot' delivering to another tank so you would have thought it was pretty obvious. I heard about how he fell out of the cab last week and shouldn't be working, and how he can't use the private health care. Blah Blah Blah... I hobbled away once he had got the plan!*

*Now I am not one to complain but I have just been told why we have so much pizza flour. There is a recipe that Domino wants to try. We have a jug on the work surface containing sultanas and cherries (not the hard ones, the ones soaked in booze!) They are covered with rum and soaking nicely. The powdered ginger and cinnamon, together with nutmeg is sitting waiting... Caribbean Chelsea buns here we come!*

*The large oven door shattered back in February, we have received many from the spares supplier mainly cream coloured ones, despite the correct model and serial number and of course, the clincher, a colour hi res photo. No, a small oven door and in cream to boot was their last effort. Italy of course have knocked off for the foreseeable, so we are using the half-sized oven. Thankfully there are only two of us!*

*Old Tiger had another box delivered, and this morning he is in the garden with a tool box making a complete din. It appears a barbeque of grand proportions has been delivered in kit form.*

*Two hours in the noise subsided and when I walked along the back path, he seemed to be near completion. This is a rather smart piece of kit, wheels, lift up lid and multiple grilles. I admit he has purchased a really good bit of kit and I congratulated him to that effect.*

*He replied proudly, that all he had to do was put on the last wheel and it was finished. I was just about to shout a warning advising the lid was up just as he tilted it to fit the wheel.*

*The screams reverberated around the close for what seemed an eternity, the lid came crashing down, right across his fingers which were gripping the frame.*

*We made a hasty exit!*

Day 52.

*I posted a photo on facebook yesterday with complete disgust. How can someone dump a plastic fuel oil tank in the road? Clearly someone with a pickup truck or a van obviously. Surely if you had to replace yours, you would set it aside until it could be disposed correctly?*

*Eventually tips will reopen and normality will return. If you have bought a new tank, it's only thirty quid more to get the council to take it away! The cheek and lack of respect for our countryside makes me a little cross!!!!!*

*All day yesterday I thought it was Bank Holiday, the turmoil going on in the world has erased the fact from my grey matter, that it's on Friday to commemorate 75 years since VE day. I have been displaying my regimental flag in the garden for some days, but I think today it's time for the Union flag to make an outing.*

*For many years I asked my dad the usual question 'what did you do in the war' as you do when you are a certain age. He was in the RAF and a butcher/chef but was somewhat vague about his war service. It transpires he joined up when he was of age and did his basic training.*

*He did his passing out parade on the eighth of May 1945! Yep, VE day! So, I can imagine he was a bit gutted he didn't get to serve in anger.*

*He did however provide meals for the aircrews doing the food drop in Holland, Operation Manna, he also went to Palestine and participated in the turmoil that went on to form the new state of Israel! He didn't do too bad! I will raise a glass to all of them who went through that important time in our history.*

*Task of the day today is to clip the wing feathers on the hens. They had eaten all their feed in their bucket yesterday afternoon, (and left untouched the tower full!)*

*They jump on the gate to shout their displeasure and offer rude gestures and stick their tongues out.*

*I went over to the feed bucket to concede defeat and one of them jumped down. This made the other go vertical, hens all over the garden. My back is not up to chasing hens at the moment, so I happened to have the landing net for my fishing trips behind the sofa. The net worked well and the squawking and shouting had the curtains twitching next door.*

*Tiger was out like a shot with his camera, taking photos of a hen in a net, head sticking out one end and feet the other! The doorbell rang a little later and a bag of sage and onion stuffing was left on the door mat! Very funny!*

Day 53.

*The Union Flag is flying outside, fluttering in the light breeze. Yesterday was a fun filled time. Tiger set up his pitch as normal but after some inaudible comment withdrew to get his mower out. Clearly, he had forgot to empty the grass box and after some frantic shoving and heaving, realised his error.*

*You may recall that it was a very windy day yesterday. Tiger pulled out his green bin and removed the grass box. He upended the box and with a huge flourish (for my benefit as he was talking to me at the time!) shook it furiously. As the dry grass came out (he mowed well over a week ago) the wind caught the whole lot had covered him in head to foot with bits of grass. Swearing in Welsh is not pretty or befitting a gentleman.*

*I crawled crying, barely able to see through an already duff sighted eye, back to my hovel for a cup of tea!*

*Some while later, the mower fired up and perfectly straight lines were being cut on the grass next door. By now his pitch looked something like one the putting greens at Carnoustie. This time he emptied the mower before putting it away.*

*When he came back five minutes later, Mrs Tiger had put the garden furniture on his pitch and was drinking tea! The golf toolkit was hurled across his patio and he settled down to look at the view in silence!*

*I posted a photo of his golf ball last night which again had been sent with some power into the field at the back of the garden. I hope he retrieves it before Vengeful woman sees it!*

*I had to write a letter yesterday. We have a wireless printer hidden under the coffee table which usually works well but not today. I will outline the angst caused by writing one letter.*

I had to send to a guy in Faversham a cheque for a refund for an event on the sixteenth of May, which sadly isn't going to happen. I have been putting this off as I need two signatures on the 'company' cheques and now only down to one signed cheque in the chequebook.

The letter was written in less than a minute and I pressed print... nothing! Printer offline, no it isn't I can see the two lights? Hand and knees time, I turned it off and on, no still offline. It then bursts into life I settle back into the sofa and when I look up, it's printed a test page! I printed the document again, nothing! Still shows offline!

Back on hands and knees! I looked at the machine and it looked back; I could see the smile on its plastic face!!!!

I did the first IA (Immediate action drill!) and cleared everything then pulled the plug out, gave it a stiff talking to and put everything back together, sat on sofa and pressed print! Nothing, it was still grinning at me from under the neat tablecloth!

Back on hands and knees, this time I carry out the second IA and pull it out and beat it furiously on the floor, helped by Rigsby who thinks it's a game!

Printer still smiling, I put it back together and returned to sofa. Gingerly I pressed print and with a sigh of relief the printer made a noise, this unfortunately was the ink carriage resetting from its beating, still offline!

I gave up, we have a monster printer in the old office which used to belong to 'one of the major insurance companies' which is reliable and used only for big print runs.

As I settled down on the office floor and plugged in the printer, I could hear laughing downstairs. In less *than a couple of minutes, I went back downstairs to find Sue in uncontrollable laughter. The pesky printer had woken up in my absence and thrown out sixteen copies of my letter!*

*I hate technology I am convinced Alexa and the printer have it in for me, Alexa has lost all my playlists and seems to be stuck on a version of Stranger on the Shore which is a lovely song played on a clarinet, but it's been on for 172 times in a row! The printer is still laughing at me and to cap it all, when we went out, I left the letter on the sofa!*

Day 54.

*Plenty of action today, MIL phoned and reported that she had torn the quick on her little toe pulling on her tights. Ever helpful, I asked why she was wearing tights this weather? Needless to say, I was spoken to in Welsh (I now know she was swearing, Tiger used the same words yesterday) Charming, but it gets better, she then cut the nail with a pair of kitchen scissors, missed and took the top of her little toe clean off! MIL pressed her 'panic button' and the kind operator suggested she elevate her leg and put a dressing over the top.*

*Good advice but oh no she kept poking it, blood all over the carpet. The priceless statement was 'You wouldn't think there was so much blood in your foot!'*

*I went on line to see if there was a care home specialising in stupidity. The only one that came up was in North Wales!*

*For a brief moment earlier my Tinnitus stopped, the sound of silence was unbelievable, I could hear a blackbird in the far distance and chainsaw miles away. As*

*I sat and contemplated my other neighbour fired up his mower! Peace shattered!*

Day 56.

*Frantic activity around here, neighbours scraping topsoil from their gardens and wheelbarrowing it away. I dare not ask! Mrs Tiger has been painting the fence and yet again, Tiger told her to put your back into it! Some people don't learn, I certainly don't, when I relayed the events the lady of the house had the radio on whilst preparing some sustenance, and thought I was telling her to 'Do you know what'!*

*After a written apology and back up from Mrs Tiger, I avoided the trip to Coventry by a whisker! There was a social distancing tea party in the close yesterday, great to see, we didn't attend as struggling with my eye today in bright sun. The TV commemoration was good and the boss as always brilliant. Some reflection and then business as usual tomorrow.*

*Below is an excerpt from my forthcoming book, Hell in my Head, due out 30<sup>th</sup> July.*

*'At dawn on the 20<sup>th</sup> May, hundreds of JU52 aircraft full of German paratroops made their way to the drop zones, as they turned west over the northern peninsular and dropped to around one thousand feet, the gunners were ready for this, but when the aircraft came into range, they were too low to engage effectively as their barrels could not be depressed that low. All they could do was watch the battle develop to the east.*

*Many Germans were killed during their descent on the drop zones as by coincidence they were landing directly on the most defended positions. When the paratroops reorganised, they moved to take the objectives to allow the main force to land safely. This was the final time parachutists were used in their traditional role.*

*General Karl Student and his men would be absorbed into the line infantry because of the high number of casualties. On the flat ground which is now Chania airport, glider troops landed and merged with the paratrooper remnants that had landed two hours earlier.*

*Gunner Aubrey Garrett was a loader in the gun troop overlooking the bay. When it became clear they could not make any difference they took to the trenches and awaited orders. The Germans advanced and because of the ground and the shape of the peninsular, there was no withdrawal route for the allies in the area.*

*When contact was made it was obvious, they could not hold out against heavily armed troops. The invading forces mortared the positions before attacking and overrunning the soldiers holding the trenches.*

*Realising they could not attack the enemy they took up defensive positions in the trenches and waited for the Germans to arrive. The positions were mortared heavily, everyone crouched down but casualties were sustained.*

*After a couple of hours, the mortars stopped and Aubrey was the first to his feet and looked over the top of the trench. At that moment one final mortar bomb fell and that was the end of him instantly. 'RIP Uncle Aubrey.*

Day 57.

*I am no fool but looking around, either I am the only sane individual, or the others look at me as the village idiot and are perfectly sane individuals, who feel sorry for me!*

*We have had a real saga over the last few days. We grew Aubergines in the garden last year and they seem to fruit well and are very colourful. As we are 'stuck in' we thought we would order some on line.*

*I found three on eBay and the despite them advertised as 'strong plugs at least three inches tall' they arrived in a plastic container amounting to one centimetre high with two leaves! I contacted the supplier and found that they have a nonstandard ruler, so my plants are what they are! Growing them on to a viable plant should take no more than three years! No moussaka from them anytime soon!*

*Domino sourced some locally, three plants grafted and individually planted, brilliant roll on supper! three plants arrived just over an inch high looking sad and by tea time two were flopped over dead! A call produced three more, this time grafted and looking strong. We had them in the spare room until the weather stabilised. They looked good growing well, and four days later are eight inches high.*

*Yesterday, I opened the Velux window to get some air but it seems I failed again. About an hour later I was alerted to some noise by the dog heading south rapidly.*

*The open window must have an invisible sign that said 'Greenfly extremely welcome' the three aubergines were covered and within an hour they were twenty-five deep all over the leaves.*

*After a while I sneaked upstairs and the sight that I witnessed will stay with me for ever! Domino was in her bikini in the shower with the aubergines, gently washing* greenfly from the leaves with warm water! You can never find a camera when you need one! Fast forward an hour, and they look good as new with the window firmly shut.

Age and experience have taught me to remain silent in these circumstances, I get the logic but the execution seemed a bit extreme. It appears I was forgiven as a superb loaf was produced a little later.

We had our second Morrison's delivery at 9pm last night. I did the maths whilst we were putting it away. If you buy a disposable carrier bag in the shop, they charge you 5p, good stuff helps focus the mind on the recycling thing which we support wholeheartedly. Indeed, we have more reusable bags than most spread around the cars and conservatory.

The best two we have a huge, we bought them in Massey's in St Lucia, they have Caribbean fruit, birds and are lime green, anyway I wander. The shop last night had every item in a 5p bag, packed individually, now that's a lot of bags. I worked out that our sixty-pound shop had forty-two pounds worth of carrier bags!

Now I am no mathematician but that's a deal! Just need how to work out how we can sell on the bags, I have been up half the night folding them nicely!

Just went to the window in the spare room and noted the padlock on the window! I was sure the aubergines were laughing at me!

Day 58.

Much hollering and clucking in the hen house this morning, they obviously need to work out the teams properly, four a side hen football doesn't work if there only four hens in total! I noted through the fence there *were three eggs in the nest, so after vaulting the fence at some cost I might add, the back is playing up today and the eye doesn't focus, so using the gate may have been more appropriate!*

*Anyway, I slid my hand into the nest, grabbed the eggs, but as I went to pull them out a big fat warm chicken stomach settled onto the back of my hand! Ok if you were expecting it, but this came as a shock, I jumped, the hen jumped and the noise is unbelievable, the neighbours 'accidently' sprayed the run with the hose to assist in the quieting down process.*

*I am standing there with three eggs, soaking wet and trying to undo the gate with one hand, whilst trying not to break the eggs!*

*The other three hens didn't help, singing 'row row row your boat' this isn't helpful or indeed clever!*

*CatMan was just in his garden chasing off a cat who was just scratching around in the newly dug cat toilet, sorry flower bed! He suggested to me if he could catch the feline it wouldn't be back in a hurry! He then proceeded to lecture me about cats in his garden. I agreed wholeheartedly and suggested it was a good idea. He was taken aback by my lack of stroppiness.*

*To placate him I told him it was cat number sixteen from around the terrace and not my cat at all! I however agree to have a word with mine and tell them to keep away!*

*I duly lined them up on the patio and proceeded to give them a good talking to, whilst wagging my finger. It seemed to work they all nodded in agreement and Cat Man was placated.*

*He went indoors and in flash, they all descended on his garden and started scraping furiously!*

*I have an ace up my sleeve, Tiger was shifting soil the other day and was using the back gates. The lovely dog from the other side was out and about running into his garden, but she disappeared into his house for quite some time! I wondered whether he has noticed anything unusual around yet? I have a photo as proof so my herd are off the hook!*

Day 59.

*We are all grownups and have the ability to think things through and make decisions based on the information presented. I think the latest guidance is clear but the media, BBC is the worst seems to be systematically putting doubts and ambiguity to the latest information.*

*The great unwashed believe the media and now we are in a state of chaos. I like being in lockdown, I don't have to mix with anyone!*

*That said, we went to Sandwich, the farm shop has this year's asparagus and Kentish new potatoes. This was the first trip out since the tenth of March, driving seemed very odd. No cars and no one in the farm shop so success all round!*

On our return CatMan was standing on our doorstep looking a tad cross, indeed he was red in the face. He had woken up to find his two new beds in the back garden had been disturbed and the soil pulled back over the path. Of course, he thought the cats had been there mob handed but I had the ace.

When I visited the little boy's room at 5:30am the blackbirds were in there getting bugs and worms and they were having a great time! I took a photo as I knew what was likely to happen.

CatMan stomped off and went to work with his broom muttering and ticking like a clock!

There was a delivery a little later, a huge cardboard box was ceremoniously dumped on the pavement outside Tiger's cave. The car was summoned and the box appeared in the garden with his toolbox about an hour later.

Again, what you would do to have a camera! The box contained a DIY lawn mower! On close inspection it was from the manufacturer 'Frisky Fox'! four hours later the oil and petrol were added and it was game on!

Tiger pulled and pulled the cord but nothing happened. I wandered down the path, as he was leaning over it very red in the face.

He showed me the built-in cup holder on the handle, very useful for adding refreshments such as a bottle of chilled Tiger beer. Clearly this was a machine built to be used semi-professionally, our man is not technically minded and when he asked me why I thought it was not starting, I suggested he turn off the choke, with a glare and a mutter, he did just that and it started first pull.

*More muttering in a foreign language and the six by ten lawn was cut in three passes. His 'frisky Fox' was built for much more than this, he had filled the two-gallon tank to the brim so it will evaporate nicely in his garden storage box. Incidentally, he had to part dismantle it again to get in to fit the box, so he could shut the door.*

*Just before dark, I was outside watering and he came out to undertake the same task. I asked if he had conquered the mower and as he turned around, he smacked his head on the hanging basket Mrs Tiger had put up earlier without his knowledge. More chuntering and indoors he went!*

Day 60.

*The excitement is building, the 'club' will be open from Wednesday, Tiger has charged his stick trailer battery, and was practising towing it around the garden wearing his studs and gloves, I expect he will be off when the sun comes up giving Mrs Tiger a well-deserved rest!*

*I am not one who normally attracts good luck, but today we have a double bubble. Our favourite wine supplier in the South of France, emailed the other day advertising the particular wine we like, is now available in a box. I always thought wine in a box was evil stuff but the research seemed to suggest this was ok. They were suppling a one litre box for £9 and free delivery.*

*We thought we would try one. It arrived this morning, six boxes containing three litre in each!!!! Using my best Google translate I spoke to them and they agreed as we were such a good customer, we could keep it.*

*Apparently, couriers from France are quite cheap but the other way are very expensive! I have eighteen litres of wine; I hope it tastes nice!*

*Half an hour later, another bonus arrives. I ordered two boxes of Felix mixed cat food, cheaper than Morrison's with free delivery. I now have eight boxes of Felix; this is 640 pouches of mixed cat food! Again, too expensive to send back, happy days.*

*When this is all over, we are having a cat food and wine party! Bring your own litter tray and wine glass!*

*I entered a survey on line to praise the efficiency of the Felix supplier. You get to win Felix!!! At the end it said to enter your gender, male female or other? I, for sheer curiosity clicked 'other' to see what options you had. twelve different versions of normal came up, now call me cynical or indeed under educated, but in my 'Biology for Idiots' class in secondary school, I am certain that they said you were born with either a thingy or a whatsit.*

*No other options, no other categories, indeed that's why the girls had separate changing facilities. Simple really, if you went by the latest madness, schools would need fourteen different types of toilet and changing facilities. This my friends are why we are doomed as a species! Pass me a Rum punch and a gender-neutral bacon sandwich!*

Day 61.

*Something went awry at the golf club today, Tiger was off at the crack and back by 9:30, he was clutching his spikes and looking very grumpy. After about an hour, Tiger and his spikes were off again with some purpose. I guess all 2000 members turned up at seven am ready to beat their sticks, social distancing meant they all had to wait their turn. I truly don't understand that game!*

*I decided to have a day off, as you do, this isolating thing is hard work. I have just finished reading a very interesting book about the tail end of World War 2 in Burma which, after my obligatory afternoon nap, led me to several thought trails.*

*We as humans seem to have the desire to travel and explore, that in itself is great but the desire to covet other nations wealth, goods and property seem to go hand in hand. Over the centuries the Romans, Persians, Turks and many more have done it to some degree (albeit slowly because they had to walk!), all in the name of trade.*

*In more recent times, the Dutch, Portuguese, French and Italians to name but a few have all land grabbed somewhere in the world. The good old British were so much different in their ambitions' yeah right!'*

*Let's randomly take a country mmm, let's go for India! Let's set up a trading company, we need to defend our trade routes, lets raise an army, ooh these nasty locals want to pinch our 'hard earned goods' let's work with the tribes to get stability, then overnight 90% of the British army is stationed in India.*

*So, it went on but my point is how rich our world is because of our perceived exploitation of others. At the time all fair and dandy, but now we are more civilised the actions of our predecessors can be seen as shameful.*

*In the British army there are still words used that have been handed down through each generation. My experience at the age of twenty-one, was that old crusty soldiers whose parents served in WW2, in Burma and*

*India and indeed the Far East would have used these words as everyday language.*

*Words such as Dhobi (Urdu for doing your washing) Wallah (Guajarati for someone employed on a specific task) Char (Used all over with minor spelling changes, from Turkey through to Arabic and of course Urdu and the many other languages in the Far East, for a nice cup of tea!)*

*These words we thought were strange but before long we used them as the norm and as new people came along, they adopted them and so on. twenty years on, a few weeks ago I heard two soldiers chatting about meeting up with a few wallahs to go for a few beers!*

*Nothing changes nothing will, we will soldier on!*

Day 62.

*Now, today has been a fun packed boredom busting time. It started early with Tiger out before 7am shifting his garden loose items, bins and crap over to our side of the garden. Shortly after, he disappears out of the front door clutching his spikes and wearing his check cap at a jaunty angle.*

*A few moments later he came round from the garage, Mrs Tiger waved him goodbye, and as she turned around, she flung her arms in the air whilst shaking her head furiously. This was all picked up on our camera which we replayed twice just to be sure!*

*The morning progressed without further interest but at 10am, a bald man in a pickup arrived and unloaded a complete fence in kit form! Tiger, I now realise was in the poo far deeper than normal.*

*Not only had he gone to poke his bats, but he had left Mrs Tiger alone to face Bald man on her own! I would not want the tongue lashing he was going to get! Clearly Bald man expected tea so shortly after, Mrs T is off up the shop and returned ten minutes later with a large carton of milk! Clearly these fence operators need a regular brew, she was not looking best pleased!*

*The digging and thumping started and we continued our hen and cat duties in the garden when Bald man called over the fence, he would be using a nail gun. He went on to explain that it sounds like a real gun so beware!*

*About ten minutes later there was a 'bang bang' a good double tap sounding indeed like a service issue browning 9mm. After a few times of this I accidently tripped over our edging low fence and did a roll over on the grass (trained to roll you know!)*

*This was greeted with amusement so every time we heard the bang we creased up and did a pretend swan song in the conservatory. This was good fun, after about half an hour all the cats had appeared and were sitting watching our stupidity, eventually they produced score cards and finally, when we decided to have a spot of lunch, the hens were also playing the game!*

*As things moved on the fence has been erected against the existing boundary, obviously CatMan didn't want to pay for the fence so Tiger arranged to do it on his side of the boundary. This was fine until the right-hand quarter turn. Now the fence has an eight-inch gap! We have a 'No Man's Land' can you imagine the solicitor's bills in fifteen years' time, arguing over who owns what!*

*Both Tiger and CatMan will be too senile to remember what they had for lunch, let alone arrangements made fifteen years before! I often wonder why we are the only sane people in a close of twelve houses, are we just unlucky?*

*Tiger returned after lunch, greeted by stony silence. He tried to redeem himself by going into the garden and try and organise Bald man, who by this time was well in the swing of things and really didn't need any directions. A few minutes later Tiger is on reluctant tea duty.*

*The moral of the story is one shouldn't arrange large tasks when 50% of the management team is not present, one of our other neighbours fell afoul of this a couple of years back and he hasn't been the same since!*

Day 63.

*Bald man arrived early this morning and got stuck into the fence. Once it took on structure and the slats were starting to fit, it did look pretty good. The 'no mans' land' was being fitted up with flood lights and guard towers, so I feel we will sleep safely in our beds from now on.*

*Tiger supervised the whole thing today and clearly; he had recovered some of his points tally. While he was putting all his tat back where it belongs, the truth dawned on him. If Mrs Tiger was to watch the golf highlights later, then the Sky dish needed to go somewhere. It was 6 inches off the ground on the old fence.*

*After checking for guards and with great bravery, he went and retrieved it. Looking relieved he proceeded to nail it halfway up the new fence at a jaunty angle. I don't have satellite TV, but I am pretty sure you have to point the disk at the satellite for it to work? Can't wait for the noise later!*

*The Sky engineer has arrived, goodness knows what that cost! From where I am sitting in the lounge, I can clearly hear the conversation, which is sort of going like this. Why did you not just undo the four bolts on the base? Now it's in bits you don't have even half a chance of sorting it without the meter. The fixings on this lovely new fence look like it's been done by a trained otter!*

*Goodness me what a site, look at all this loose cable not a clip in sight.... tut tut. Meanwhile Tiger is spluttering and stammering with his head down! I think he will sneak off and beat his sticks soon!*

*After the dust has settled, he is now sitting in his pants reading the golf weekly on his newly private patio! except that from our second-floor window you can see everything!)*

Day 64.

*Gosh I am tired; I was up at 04:30 making sandwiches and goodies for the event of the year. Sue's birthday today, Abs and Tom came over at midday for a LOOOOONG lunch. This was a complete surprise to her and a real struggle to keep it quiet.*

*The shopping came last night and the fridge was rammed, I couldn't find any of the stuff I had carefully squirreled away yesterday. I had to tell a porky too, my back was so bad I couldn't join in on the daily Rigsby walk!*

*Off she went at 11:30 with Rigs, I furiously got out the tables, one on the top patio and the other on the lower* one. Two table cloths, plates and glasses and a rather smart bottle of fizzy pop! (Thanks Stu and Jacqui!). The guests arrived and the party commenced. Tiger and co were looking at us a little puzzled, as we had to shout at each other for two hours down the garden!

I even chalked direction of movement arrows so we didn't all bump as the toileting began!

Tiger was still in trouble this morning. Now his work in the garden has been approved and signed off as fit for purpose, it was time for a trip to the garden centre. Off they went and before he went to the end of the road he was back! Car abandoned in middle of the road with doors flung open, Mrs T was red with rage, Tiger had forgotten his wallet (again) and was sent in to collect it.

It was like the 'walk of shame' he slunk indoors shaking his head whilst Mrs T kept up the 'friendly banter' from the front of the car. £5 quid says he is off to the golf at sunrise before she awakes from her slumber in the morning!

After all the charging about I now really have a sore back!

Day 65.

I took the plunge today and decided to venture out again, seems the garden centres are open and shops are getting back to normal stock levels etc. The reality is I think we can venture out and be something near normal. I don't mind standing in queues with two metre gaps, at least you don't have to engage random strangers in drivel!

We consider we are no longer trapped indoors so the daily blog will cease (Unless we get locked down *again if it returns) Thank you for reading the boredom buster, and hope it kept your spirits up in these difficult times!*

*One final comment on the blog is that 100% normality has returned is the 'stick test', since Wednesday, Tiger has been gone well before seven am dressed for a fancy-dress party with his cap at a jaunty angle! Stay safe everyone!*

Glossary of terms

A. Amazon Alexa, smart device used for playing music, games and searching facts on the internet.
AWOL, Military shorthand for absent without leave.

B. Bacon Grill. This is processed bacon similar to spam, again a breakfast option (the only option!) in an army ration pack. Most supermarkets sell it and it tastes just the same as it always did, although of course I am not wet and cold nor been awake for three days.

C. Cheese possessed is a colloquial term for tinned processed cheese. It has a shelf life of about ten years and the staple of many a 10-man army ration pack.
Crud, general slang term for muck, residue or a sticky mess.

D. Dyson, a type of vacuum cleaner extremely good suction and lightweight.
Doodoo, a slang term for being in the worst possible trouble you can imagine.

H. Holliers, this is a slang term for holiday used more often these days in the world of text/phone speak

L. Levi Roots, TV chef from Jamaica. Famous for his reggae reggae sauce

M. MIL, Mother in Law!
Monopoly. Board game made by Waddington's for budding property magnates!

Morrisons, UK national supermarket chain.

P. Punji stick, this is a pointed stick either singly or in groups. They were popular during the Vietnam war and used by the North Vietnamese forces to create effectively a terror weapon. They could be well hidden and inflict terrible injuries. Also, a forerunner of biological warfare, the tips would be smeared with poison or excrement which did its worst some three weeks after coming to contact.
Pets are Robbers, local slang for the chain 'Pets at Home'
Patrixbourne, a small village near Canterbury.

R. RMP, Royal Military Police, UK military police force.

S. Stazi, State security service in Cold War East Germany, known for sneaking about to catch perceived miscreants.
Sellotape, manufacturers brand name for a clear tape, glued on one side, used mostly in the wrapping of my Christmas and birthday presents.

T. Titting about. Kentish/military term for randomly messing about in a random or disorganised fashion.
Tinnitus, incurable medical condition where the suffer hears noises such as humming, gurgling or whistling.

Tee, A plastic pin with a cup for placing a golf ball. Used when taking the initial shot from the green!
Training area, areas of land either owned by the military or leased from farmers. They are used to conduct realistic training without frightening the general public!

V. Vickyverky, a local Kentish term to mean vice versa
VE day, Victory in Europe day, celebrated on the 8<sup>th</sup> May every year since 1945.

**About the author**

     John Bennett was born in Canterbury and educated locally. In 1988 John left the motor trade and joined Sun Alliance insurance as a staff motor engineer where he progressed via a convoluted route to become a team leader of motor engineers in the North of England, Scotland and Northern Ireland.

     John took early retirement in 2013 and is involved with the Princess of Wales's Royal Regiment (PWRR) Regimental association, assisting with its growth and development. John is also passionate about the Regimental museum in Dover Castle and works as a volunteer assisting with outreach projects and doing talks and tours.

     John is also on the Regimental heritage committee representing the TA and Army reserve. In addition, John is the mental Health Champion in the regimental association and is a qualified mental health first aider. This is the fourth book John has written, the memoirs of his twenty-seven years serving the country, and Hell in my Head, the story of three generations of family who have suffered mental health problems as a result of conflict, and memories of a Kentish village. Childhood memories of growing up in a small village

Acknowledgements
I would like to thank my wife Sue for the patience and sympathy extended towards me as an unintentional victim. Dave Stevenson for his wisdom and confidence and Fiona and Sean Doherty for the common sense. Gail Arnold for suggesting the title and finally Jessica Hayes, for providing the front cover and the illustrations

Disclaimer.
The majority of events mentioned actually took place although somewhat embellished. Characters and nicknames feature mostly within the bounds of my head and don't reflect on any of our lovely neighbours.

Printed in Great Britain
by Amazon